Forming Bible Study Groups

Steve Clapp
and
Gerald W. Peterson

faithQuest
Elgin, Illinois

Forming Bible Study Groups

Copyright © 1990 by *faithQuest,* a Division of Brethren Press, 1451 Dundee Avenue, Elgin, IL 60120

Scripture quotations are from the Revised Standard Version of the Bible, copyrighted 1946, 1952, 1971, 1973, 1977 by the National Council of Churches of Christ in the U.S.A., Division of Education and Ministry.

Cover Design by Jeane Healy

Library of Congress Cataloging-in-Publication Data

Clapp, Steve
    Forming Bible study groups/Steve Clapp, Gerald Peterson.
           p. cm.
    ISBN 0-87178-293-6
    1. Bible—Study. 2. Church group work. I. Peterson, Gerald.
    II. Title.
    BS603.C52 1990
    268—dc20   90–40628 CIP

Manufactured in the United States of America

Contents

*"In the beginning
was the Word
and the Word was with God"*
John 1:1

1

In the Beginning

"When I feel ready to lose my sanity, I go back to the twenty-third Psalm. Those words bring me so much comfort."

"The Bible isn't just another book. I can't explain it, but the words take on a life of their own. I can feel myself being changed as I read the Bible, and the change is for the better."

"I believe the Bible really has the answers to the major questions of our age, but it isn't easy to be sure. Some people have quoted Scripture to justify slavery, war, and other atrocious practices. How can you really understand the Bible?"

"I don't think the Bible's purpose is to answer our questions as much as to ask us questions. I'm pushed to examine my life and society in the light of the Bible."

Do those words sound familiar? The first statement comes from a woman who does not belong to a church, the second from a church active teenage girl, the third from a man who is very active in a local church, and the fourth from a seminary professor. You've probably heard similar statements in your own church and community.

People are fascinated by the Bible. We live in a fast paced, technologically sophisticated society but the ancient words of the Bible still communicate contemporary reality. Human nature has not changed, God has not changed and the Bible's relevance for us has not changed.

In a survey of teenagers conducted in the late nineteen eighties, two-thirds of them wanted to know more about the Bible. What makes the results especially fascinating is that the study included many teens who are not active in a local church! About sixty percent of the adults responding to a similar survey indicated the same desire.

So why aren't our churches overrun with young people and adults studying the Bible? For three reasons (at least):

1. People make most decisions in response to immediate pressures rather than from an overall view of their lives. A survey like the one just described pushes people to think about what's most important in their lives. In this process, God and what the Bible teaches about God

often emerge as primary concerns. In the midst of hectic daily lives many people do not give the same thoughtful consideration to how they use their time.

2. Schedules really are a problem for many people. Adult males today presumably have more leisure time than in previous generations but they also have more options to fill that time. Adult females today are far more likely to work than in previous generations, but they still carry primary responsibility for the household (equality in household tasks has not accompanied equality in employment!). Children and teenagers have ever increasing options for evening and weekend activities.

3. The fear of looking foolish keeps some people away from organized Bible study. People do feel the Bible is important and that they should know more than they do about the Bible. They may fear looking foolish in group discussions and thus avoid such opportunities. Many adults still carry scars from embarrassing educational experiences as children and youth; they don't want to repeat those experiences as adults.

Our strategies for involving people in Bible study must recognize those barriers. We need to help people by:

- Keeping them aware of ultimate concerns, of what really is most important in life.
- Providing opportunities at times that are as convenient as possible for people and involving them in determining those times.
- Creating groups that help people feel comfortable and secure in study and sharing rather than groups that put people on the spot and embarrass them. The next section on "Forming New Groups" gives detailed advice on how to accomplish this.

The Bible communicates God's continuing Word for our lives. Through our study of the printed words on the pages of the Bible, God's living Word comes through, touching our lives at points of need, confronting us, challenging us, healing us, making us whole. The words of Scripture communicate the living Word, Jesus Christ. And those words take on special meaning when shared in a group setting. Exciting things happen in the lives of people as they study the Bible.

2

Forming New Groups

When a new Bible study group is formed in the church, the customary approach is to announce the group from the pulpit and put notices in the church bulletin and newsletter. These steps generally result in something less than the desired response. The approach recommended here has been used successfully in churches of all sizes and denominations:

1. **Form a planning committee to start a new group** (or several groups!). The committee doesn't have to be large—two or three people are sufficient. What is important is that not all the responsibility be carried by a single person.

2. **Make a list of people the planning committee members know who might be interested in Bible study.** Think about people who are naturally inclined toward Bible study but also think about people who could benefit from such a group even though they may not seem so inclined. If you are planning neighborhood Bible study groups, then think of people who have no church home who might respond positively.

3. **Then phone or visit each of those people.** Tell them why you feel a Bible study group is so important and encourage them to be part of it. Don't use high pressure (that always backfires), but do make it clear you would like them in the group. Ask four questions of each person:

- What would you like to study? If you have specific resources in mind give them a choice of initial topics.
- When could you meet with a group? Some very successful groups meet at times like 6 a.m., 6 p.m., and 10 p.m. Responses will usually be more traditional but don't exclude any possibility.
- Who else would you like to see in the group? Get the names, addresses, and phone numbers of other persons who could benefit from the experience and whom the person you are visiting would like to have in the group.
- Would you like to have a single teacher/leader for the group, or should the group share leadership? If the persons would prefer a

single leader, find out whom those persons would suggest. This may help you in leadership recruitment. (Don't ask this question if you already have a leader in mind or recruited!)

If you talk with someone who is uncertain about the group, still be sure to get answers to the four questions. Later, if the group established meets the needs of those who responded to the questions, you may find the person willing to participate. The questions provide a way of helping the person begin thinking about a group and can slowly move that person toward a commitment to a group.

4. **Recruit a teacher or coordinator for the group.** If the potential members contacted prefer shared leadership, you only need a coordinator for the group. A coordinator assumes responsibility for seeing that a leader is available each week and that necessary group tasks are accomplished (ordering resource materials, contacting absent members, seeing that refreshments are provided, etc.).

5. **Then the coordinator or teacher makes the following decisions,** based on the suggestions of the persons contacted in the third step:

- Meeting day and time.
- Date to have the first session.
- Meeting place.
- The initial topic for study.

6. **Make return contacts to all those contacted in step three and any additional persons who have been identified.** Communicate the information about the initial meeting and ask if you can order a resource book or study guide for that person.

Make your initial order for materials based on those responses.

Note: Some Bible study groups use no study guide except the Bible. That approach can be a good one if the teacher has good familiarity with the Bible and knowledge of different teaching methods. Most of us need a guide which gives more background on Scripture and discussion/activity suggestions. If you are not ordering materials, then simply ask the persons called in this step to mark the date of the first session on their calendars.

7. **Begin additional publicity.** You already have the core for your group (or groups) and can reach additional people. Depending on the kind of group you are starting, you can consider:

- Fliers in the neighborhood (for neighborhood groups).
- More phone calls or visits (by those who will be in the group).
- Church bulletin announcements.

- Church newsletter announcements.
- A minute speaker at morning worship services encouraging people to join the group.
- A special mailing to church members.

Note that in this approach you are beginning traditional group publicity after you already have a core membership for the group (or groups). Of course, depending on the schedule for newsletter articles and other publicity, you may need to run steps six and seven concurrently.

8. Make final reminder calls to group members before the first meeting. If you have resource materials, deliver the guide or book to each person and give a personal reminder of the first meeting.

9. Follow up with positive encouragement to any who indicated interest but failed to be present for the first session.

What size should a group be? The answer is . . . it depends! Groups as small as three or four people have met successfully each week for years. Some group models which anticipate lots of opinion sharing and group discussion work best with no more than ten or twelve people in a group.

In general most classes or groups will not grow much larger than twenty-five persons unless one of two criteria is met: (1) The group has a dynamic teacher/leader and relies more on lecture/discussion than on sharing/ discussion. OR (2) The group frequently divides into smaller sharing/discussion groups.

As a general rule, ten or twelve regular attenders are about right for a single group. If you have the wonderful problem of more people than that, you can handle it by starting additional groups or by doing more small group activities within the large group. Note that the recruitment strategies mentioned can be used to establish more than one group at the same time. Remember, however, that you need a teacher or coordinator for each group.

Short term or long term? There are pluses and minuses to both short and long term groups. Persons who have not been part of a group before are usually more open to participation in a short term group (which has a clear beginning and ending). Neighborhood groups which seek to involve nonmembers should generally be short term. The same is true of groups at the church which are focused on reaching nonmembers or members who have not been previously involved in study groups. Groups which are for active members may well be long term or may become long term in response to the interests of group members. Neighborhood groups composed of church families may begin as short term groups but become long term as people gain from the study and personal sharing.

3

Maintaining Healthy Group Life

The suggestions which follow can help you create a group or class climate which will be pleasant and stimulate meaningful discussion. You may not follow every suggestion, but you should give serious consideration to most of them. These are based on observations of many successful Bible study classes and groups.

1. Offer refreshments! A cup of coffee or tea helps set an informal, pleasant atmosphere for a group. You can have cookies or donuts if you wish. Obviously a different drink should be substituted for children and youth. Adults might consider alternatives to coffee or tea like cider, lemonade, or hot chocolate, depending on the season.

2. Don't meet longer than an hour without a short break that lets people move around, refill their coffee, go to the restroom, etc. The break should normally be between five and fifteen minutes in length.

3. Unless your group is very large, meet around a table or in a circle. People feel more comfortable in such settings and find it easier to share.

4. To get more people involved in sharing their opinions and ideas, try strategies like these:

5. Go around the table or circle and ask everyone to share his or her opinion on a particular topic.

6. Divide into pairs or triads to discuss certain topics or research certain biblical passages.

7. Take hand-counts to identify group sentiment. How many feel the elder son was justified in being upset by all the attention given the prodigal son? How many disagree?

8. Divide into small groups (five to six people in a group) to discuss particular questions about a biblical passage.

9. When giving instructions to pairs, triads, or small groups, write a summary of the instructions on chalkboard or newsprint so they are easily seen. If pairs, triads, or small groups are to report back to the total group, have newsprint and markers available for them

to record their information or opinions. The newsprint makes it easier to share with the total group.

10. Homework can be all right, but don't assume that everyone will have done it and don't make people feel guilty for failing to do it. Do encourage personal study between meeting times. Positive encouragement is fine, but you don't want people to feel tension in a church setting.

11. Have group members agree that what is shared about personal problems in the group stays in the group. You may well have people open their hearts about problems with parents, children, spouses, friends, employers, or employees. Cherish that sharing and reinforce it by keeping such matters confidential. Group members should be reminded of this periodically.

12. Start and end each meeting with prayer. One of those prayers should be reasonably succinct, but the other may be more open-ended—giving group members opportunity to lift up special concerns in prayer.

13. If you have a short term group, have a special meal or party near the end of your study. If you have a long term group, consider such an event at least a couple of times a year.

14. Have a plan to follow-up on absences. When someone misses a session without the group being aware of the reason, be sure that a phone call is made letting that individual know he or she was missed. If two or more sessions are missed without an explanation being known, a visit should be made to the group member's home. Absence always means something: sickness, family problems, work problems, hurt feelings, changed priorities, etc. **People need to know they are missed. The group needs to know if something that happened in the group is keeping a member away.**

15. Be sure visitors and new group members are introduced and helped to feel part of the group. If you are using a study guide, provide a copy for the new member.

16. When a long term group breaks for a holiday or the summer, have phone calls made to remind everyone of the next regular meeting.

17. Depending on the amount of meeting time available, start or end your group by letting members share joys and concerns. Depending on the size of your group, this sharing can take between fifteen and forty-five minutes. Joys and concerns is an open time in which group members share both the *joys* ("I'm a new grand-mother!" or "I got an A in Algebra.") and concerns ("My neighbor has cancer." or "My husband could lose his job.") of the week.

Others can respond in a supportive way, and this kind of sharing helps people draw closer to one another. It also helps you relate Bible study to the daily lives of group members. This strategy is not a good idea if your meeting time is very limited. The first few times you share joys and concerns you will probably only have five or ten minutes of sharing but this will change dramatically as trust develops in your group.

18. Decide whether to ask all people to use the same biblical translation or different translations. Following along while others read is easier when everyone has the same translation, but a diversity of translations can enhance your discussion by shedding new light on a biblical passages. You do need to make a clear distinction on what your group policy will be.

4

An Overview of
Teaching/Learning Methods

Most Bible study classes and groups are primarily conducted by a leader who presents certain information to the group and then poses questions for discussion. In "Maintaining Healthy Group Life," several suggestions were made for having more people share opinions and participate in discussion. Now we want to consider some additional suggestions for group leadership and a few teaching methods that aren't so commonly used.

1. In asking questions about a biblical passage, begin with specific questions and move to more general questions. In discussing the story of the Good Samaritan, first ask questions like: "In response to what concern did Jesus tell this parable?" (To tell who one's neighbor is). "What do we know about the Samaritan from this parable?" (He traveled, he had enough money to pay for the injured man's care, he had compassion, etc.). Then move to questions like: "What is the meaning of this parable for our lives today?" The specific questions are easier to answer and help people become comfortable before tackling questions dealing with larger issues.

2. Have group members brainstorm words to describe a particular character or situation. For example, one group described Hosea as forgetful, intelligent, committed, slightly strange, deceived, forgiving, patient.

3. Ask group members to tell how they would respond if they were in the same situation as a person in biblical times. For example: "How would you respond if you had been in the church at Philippi and received Paul's letter?" "How would you have lived the rest of your life if you were the demoniac Jesus healed in Matthew 9:32–33?"

4. Ask group members to tell how they think a particular biblical character would respond to a contemporary situation. "What would Paul say about the presence of so many different denomi-

nations today?" "What do you think Micah would say about nuclear weapons?"

5. If you have access to a video camera, make a group video which relates a biblical story or discusses a contemporary situation in light of the Bible. This can be an exciting activity that can be shared with other groups in the church.

6. Conduct surveys to find out what group members (or even your whole church) think about a particular issue or concern.

7. Do a newspaper search relative to a biblical passage. Have a supply of newspapers and have group members search through them to find contemporary situations related to the biblical passage.

8. Make crossword puzzles for your class or group. It isn't hard to do! Generally the easiest way to begin is with one fairly long word running across. Then build other answers and questions from that.

9. Have group members use artistic media to express their feelings or insights on a particular biblical passage or contemporary concern. We generally think about artistic expression in terms of children and young people, but many adults also enjoy the process. You can have people:
   a. Make collages (glue pictures and words from magazines and newspapers to posterboard or newsprint).
   b. Make murals to tell a biblical story.
   c. Do finger painting (especially good for expressing emotions).
   d. Make clay sculpture.
   e. Make puppets to retell a biblical story.
   f. Write songs or poems.

10. Role play a particular situation. Assign parts and have people take on that role, responding as they think that person would have.

11. Make attitude scales for your group. Let one end of the scale be low agreement with a particular statement and the other end of the scale be high agreement. An X can be used to mark where a person feels along the scale. For example:

    a. I think Judas was deeply ashamed of what he did.

    _____

    Low   High

b. I think Judas was forgiven for his sins.

_____

Low   High

c. I think I've betrayed Jesus as badly as Judas did.

_____

Low   High

For a different approach, put a big line on the floor in the middle of your meeting room; have people physically stand at the point on the line which expresses their feelings.

1. Rewrite a biblical passage in their own words.
2. Make outlines of biblical passages, identifying the major points.
3. Use biblical commentaries and dictionaries to study the background of a particular biblical passage. The leader of the group should do this every week unless using good resource material which provides this information.
4. Study how several biblical versions handle the translation of a biblical passage. The King James, New King James, Revised Standard, New Revised Standard, Good News, Living Bible, and New English Bible all provide interesting variations. The differences can be especially striking with some of Paul's letters.

5

Children, Youth, Adults, and Families

The instructions in this guide are especially applicable to youth and adult groups but can also be used with groups of children and with families. Here are some additional comments by age level.

Children

1. The curriculum you use with children is especially important. We recommend that you use curriculum developed by your own denomination or by a publisher with a similar theological perspective. Most of us need the help of curriculum suggestions in working with children. The curriculum will provide a variety of methods helpful in teaching children.
2. In any study with children, consistency of leadership is especially important. Resist the temptation to rotate leaders. A team teaching approach in which two or more persons share leadership is very appropriate and can give the flexibility needed when a member of the team must be absent.
3. Traditionally, children's Bible study has included a great deal of memorization. There is some evidence that verses learned during childhood are retained through the course of life and may give comfort and help in time of needs. Don't focus so much on memorization, however, that application and understanding are neglected. It is more important for children to understand the Bible and its meaning for their lives.
4. Children need help learning some basics about the Bible: how it came into being, what the major divisions are, how to look up biblical passages. Good curriculum materials provide help in doing this (appropriate to each age level) but you should supplement the curriculum material when necessary.
5. Although it is true for any age, it is especially true for children that relationships with teachers and other adult leaders are extremely important. Children will remember the love and concern with which they've been treated long after they've forgotten what

they were taught. **The Bible comes to life through the lives of loving teachers.**

Youth

1. Youth are especially interested in the relationship between the Bible and their daily lives. Emphasize this in your work with them.
2. The video making approach mentioned in "An Overview of Teaching/ Learning Methods" is especially effective with teenagers. Some youth study groups have had great fun making a series of videos on the Bible to share with children's classes. This is a wonderful way to make the Bible come alive with teens and to help children's groups as well.
3. A Joys and Concerns time (see "Maintaining Healthy Group Life") works especially well with teenagers.

Adults

1. Adults often respond positively to neighborhood groups meeting in homes. The warmth of the household setting can contribute much to the study atmosphere.
2. Young couples, young singles, and young families with children have busy schedules but can often be persuaded to make a Bible study group a priority once they have had a positive short term experience. Your best approach in reaching young adults (whether parents or not) is to start with a short term group.
3. It's also good to mix generations in some adult study groups. Younger adults and older adults can learn a great deal from each other.
4. Some churches have found that young adult attendance at mid-week study groups increases dramatically when child care is provided.
5. The weeks immediately before Christmas and immediately before Easter have traditionally been the most successful times for short term adult Bible study. The coming of Christmas and Easter makes people more open to a period of study. The weeks before Easter have the added advantage of not being filled with as many competing seasonal activities (office parties, shopping, etc.).

Families

Families can enjoy studying the Bible together—in the home or as part of an intergenerational church or neighborhood group. If you start family groups, keep these factors in mind:

1. Encourage artistic expression. Children learn especially well by working with their hands. Adults and youth usually start the artistic work to help the children and then find themselves caught up with equal enthusiasm.

2. Use drama: role-playing, acting out biblical situations, making videos. Remember that the attention span of children is limited—after extended periods of reading or discussion without movement or a break, you will lose their attention. Use a variety of teaching methods.

6

Covenant Bible Studies

We especially want you to know about a series of Bible study materials called the Covenant Bible Study Series. These are designed for small group relational Bible study. Relational Bible study is designed to encourage people to share their observations with one another and to develop an atmosphere of trust within the study group. This approach does a great deal to make the Bible come to life in the midst of the group and in the hearts of the participants.

There are ten sessions in each Covenant study, so the materials can be used for short term groups or for a ten week study as part of a long term group. Each session includes help in:

Preparation: The reading of Scripture and thinking about Scripture which are necessary before probing the meaning and application of a particular passage.

Understanding: The background of the biblical passage necessary to understand what it means to those who first heard or read the words and then help in applying those words to our own time. This biblical and contextual material is helpful for both leaders and learners.

Discussion and Action: Suggested discussion questions and projects for group use. These provide the basis for most of the activity by a class or group.

The Covenant Bible Study Series provides carefully designed studies, and we recommend them to you:

Disciplines for Spiritual Growth by Karen Peterson Miller
Love and Justice by Eva O'Diam
The Life of David by Larry Fourman
The Lord's Prayer by Mary Sue Rosenberger
The Presence and the Power by Robert Dell
Psalms by John David Bowman
Sermon on the Mount by Robert C. Bowman

For more information, contact *faithQuest*, 1451 Dundee Avenue, Elgin, IL 60120.

7

Sharing Time and Prayer Time

Many Bible study groups which meet at times other than Sunday morning find it meaningful to spend two hours together, using the first hour for sharing and prayer, and then the second hour for Bible study. They find that the Bible study is enhanced by the sharing and that the sharing time more strongly bonds the group together. Other groups prefer to begin with Bible study and then use the second hour for sharing and prayer. You can, of course, modify these suggested times taking, for example, thirty minutes for sharing and an hour for Bible study or forty-five minutes for each.

The time of sharing and prayer can be structured in many ways depending on the needs of your group. It will usually include these elements:

- An opening time of prayer.
- Sharing of needs or concerns of group members.
- Coming to God in prayers of intercession, prayers of thanksgiving, and prayers of confession.
- Discussion (if time permits) of a topic of importance to group members or sharing in an exercise to help members grow closer to one another.
- A closing time of prayer.

Some groups like to use a scriptural benediction or a song as part of their closing ritual. Some songs that have been used:

- "God Be With You Till We Meet Again"
- "They'll Know We Are Christians By Our Love"
- "Weave, Weave"
- "Blest Be The Tie That Binds"

Your group may wish to develop its own statement of purpose for the sharing and prayer time. The statement can help give a focus for the use of that time. For example:

Our group covenants together to:

- pray for one another and actively seek ways to help one another
- become more aware of the world in which we live and the needs of that world

- grow closer to God and to one another

Members may also find it useful to agree on a few guidelines for group participation. For example:

- We covenant together to attend every meeting and to notify the group coordinator in advance if possible) when we will be absent. The notification saves other group members anxiety about the person who is absent.
- We covenant together to hold in confidence whatever is shared in the group. We want this to be a group in which we feel safe to share our deepest thoughts and feelings.
- We covenant together to respect and love one another even when we have differences of opinion. Our differences are part of our uniqueness as God's children.

Many groups find it helpful to share both joys and concerns: joys shared and thanksgiving expressed to God for what has happened pesonally in the family, the church, the community, or the world; sorrows and concerns shared and brought to prayer for things that have happened to persons and in the wider world.

Another approach to weekly sharing is simply for each person to respond to a question like: Have you sensed God at work in your life this week?

The undirected sharing by group members (Joys and Concerns or a similar approach) will sometimes take most of your meeting time. When it does not, use other activities or discussion topics to help members draw closer to one another and to God. The pages which follow provide many suggested activities and topics. Note especially the "Introductory Group Activities." These activities are especially valuable during your first several sharing and prayer times.

Group Size

As already discussed, successful Bible study groups can range in size from very small to very large. If your group wants to have a sharing and prayer time, it is crucial that the group be no more than eight to twelve people as it meets for that purpose. If your Bible study group is larger, you want to divide into smaller groups for the sharing and prayer time. The composition of those smaller groups should remain the same each week so members have opportunity to become comfortable with one another. You will occasionally need to make changes and to integrate new members into existing groups, but you want as much continuity as possible.

8

Introductory Group Activities

Whether your group meets for Bible study only or for a time of sharing and prayer, you will want to use some activities which help members learn more about each other. Trust obviously must be built over time, but trust becomes easier as we know more about each other.

The following activities have all been used successfully in Bible study groups. You can select ones to use with your group, and the ideas here may help you develop other activities of your own. These activities are intended for youth and adult groups. Some can be modified for family groups and children's groups.

1. Have each group member draw a floor plan of the first home he or she remembers. Divide into pairs, and have each person explain the floor plan and describe life in that house to his or her partner. When you come back as a total group, have each person share what was learned about the partner through the exercise. You may wish to share a sample drawing with your group. (Straight lines and neatness are irrelevant to this exercise!)

2. If your group is meeting nearing a holiday, have each member share a favorite childhood memory of that holiday. (This works very well for Easter, Thanksgiving, and Christmas. It doesn't work so well for Labor Day or President's Day!)

3. Have each group member describe the three smells remembered best from childhood and why those memories remain. For example: "The sweet smell of my Grandfather from his pipe tobacco ... The delicious aroma of bread in my mother's oven ... The smell of the ocean when we went to the beach ..."

4. Have each group member describe the three sounds remembered best from childhood and why those memories remain. For example: "The sound of my mother starting the car before going to work ... The sound of a fire in the fireplace ... The sound of one of our many cats purring ...

5. Have each group member share his or her favorite passage of Scripture and the reason for liking that passage so much. In a typical

group, you will have many people identify Psalm 23 or the Lord's Prayer. Don't worry about the repetition. The reasons for the choices will differ and will help you better understand one another.

6. Have each person write the answers to the following questions on a note card:

- What is your favorite color?
- What is your favorite movie?
- What is your favorite passage of Scripture?
- If money were no object, what kind of car would you buy?
- If you could magically change one thing about your appearance, what would it be?

Collect and shuffle the note cards. Select a card and read the answer to the first question. See if the group can guess the identity of the person. If not, read the answer to the second question and have the group guess again. If the group has not guessed after the answer to the fifth question, the card's author will have to identify himself or herself. Continue through the cards in the same way. Obviously, guessing becomes easier as more authors are identified, but the sharing still helps people learn more about each other. All answers should be read—even if the person's identity is guessed almost immediately.

7. Have each person answer these questions: "If you weren't here tonight, where would you be and what would you be doing? Why did you choose to come to this group?" This exercise works especially well with people who have crowded, busy lives and who may have mixed feelings about time taken for the Bible study group. This kind of sharing usually helps people feel better about the decision to join the group.

8. Have each person share two or three things which he or she especially hopes to gain through participating in the group. You may want to gain through participating in the group. You may want to list these on newsprint and refer to them again at a future session.

9. If everyone in your group belongs to the church, have each person describe a communion or eucharist which was especially meaningful.

9

Other Sharing Group Activities

The previous section included activities which are especially helpful in the first few weeks of sharing group meetings. The activities in this section can be used whenever you like as part of a sharing group meeting. These can supplement your regular group sharing and help stimulate discussion. Some of these activities can also be used as part of regular Bible study time (especially activities 4, 5, 8, 9, and 16–30).

1. Ask group members to identify one or two personal goals for growth in the spiritual life. Have them write the same goal(s) on two note cards. Then give each group member an envelope. One card should be sealed in the envelope with the member's name written on it. Then collect the envelopes. Each member should keep the other note card as a continuing reminder of the goal(s) selected. Explain that you will distribute the envelopes at a meeting in five weeks. The members can look again at the goal(s) then and determine progress. Let members talk as much as they want about the goals selected, but don't put pressure on anyone to share.

2. Make a list of the birthdays of group members (month and day—not year!). Celebrate the birthdays of group members on the meeting closest to each person's birthday. The celebration may be as simple as the sharing of a prayer of thanks for that person's birth, or it may be as elaborate as a full party with refreshments. Consider making the focus of your sharing a discussion of that person's favorite biblical passage or a topic chosen by that person.

3. Have group members make small crosses out of burlap. The crosses can be put on clothing or fastened to a larger worship center cross. Explain: "Burlap is an imperfect material. It has a rough texture and is an unrefined fabric, yet each strand is unique, and the strands strengthen one another. The result is a symbol of great love." (The burlap cross is the symbol of People of the Covenant, a program developed by the Church of the Brethren.) Then talk about the ways in which the group is like the burlap cross. You may want to share in the song "Weave, Weave" by Rosemary Crow which can be found in the

Outdoor Ministry songbook, *Come Join the Circle*, published in 1989 by Brethren Press.

4. Have group members share examples of promises: Which were made to them and broken;

- Which were made to them and kept even though with great difficulty;
- Which they made and were later unable to keep;
- Which they made and kept with great difficulty.

Then talk about God's promises to us. You may especially want to look at the covenant made after the flood; see Genesis 9:12–17.

5. To do this activity, you need a container in which you can safely have a small fire. During a time of silence, have group members write down the sins for which they feel special need of forgiveness. Assure them that the sins will not be read aloud or shown to anyone. Have members fold the papers; then collect and burn the sins as a symbol of God's full forgiveness of our transgressions. Read a passage of scripture like 1 John 2:12b ("Your sins are forgiven for his sake"). Talk together about God's forgiveness, and have a time of prayer.

6. Have group members make "faith shields" by drawing a shield on a sheet of paper and dividing it into four sections. Have them write in each quadrant:

Color symbolizing your relationship with God	A question of struggle in your present faith life
A gift God has given you	How you are using God's gift

Then talk together about the shields. You may wish to read Ephesians 6:10–20 which tells us to "put on the whole armor of God." Discuss these questions: Against what do we need protection? How does God protect us? Why are struggles inevitably part of the spiritual life?

7. Ask each group member what he or she would do if given a million dollars tax free.

8. Sing the familiar song "Amazing Grace," read Romans 5:1–5, and then talk about the meaning of grace:

- What do you think God's grace is?
- When have you felt especially touched by God's grace?
- When has another person helped you experience God's grace?

9. Read Proverbs 30:18–19, and then talk about mysteries:

- Share favorite mystery stories from childhood. Share recent mysteries group members have read. Share recent mysteries from television shows or motion pictures.
- Why are we so intrigued by mysteries?
- Why has God left us with so many mysteries about the world?
- Why are mysteries an important part of the life of faith?
- What would you say is the central mystery of the Christian faith?

10. Use masking tape to fasten a piece of paper on the back of each group member. Then have the group members write positive comments on one another's backs—identifying the gifts each person has. People have a good time milling about as they write on each other, and they are often deeply moved when they read all that has been written.

11. Do a "gift bombardment." Have one person at a time sit in a chair in the center of the group. Then other group members share aloud the gifts and strengths of that person.

This exercise is similar to that in activity ten above, but the focus is on one person at a time. If group members are a little awkward about personal sharing, activity ten is an easier one to use. Groups which have been in existence a longer time will deeply appreciate activity eleven.

12. Have group members share what things they think about when their "minds drift." This could include thoughts while waiting in a traffic jam, waiting in a doctor's office, taking a walk, or just before going to sleep at night. Keith Miller has suggested that those thoughts may sometimes be clues to what we worship instead of God. Do members agree with Miller's suggestion? Why, or why not?

13. People often try to control one another in subtle (and not so subtle) ways. That control often involves withholding affection, pouting, or sharing resentment when another person doesn't do what is wanted. Have group members share ways in which other people try to control their behavior. Have those who are willing share ways in which they have tried to control the behavior of others. What differences do we notice between a person who simply requests a particular action on our part and a person who attempts to manipulate us into doing what he or she wants regardless of our feelings? How did Christ motivate people to follow him?

14. We notice in the Gospels that Jesus treated women with respect and equality which were unusual in that day. In our own time we continue to struggle with male and female roles in society. Have members share ways in which male and female roles are changing. In

what ways do we still lack true equality of opportunity for both men and women? What struggles do group members have over male and female roles? How do the Gospels help us in determining how to treat all people?

15. Use some sharing and prayer sessions to focus on a particular problem in your community or in the world. Have one or two volunteers do research on the problem and report back to the group. Once factual information has been shared, the focus of group discussion should be on a Christian view of the problem and the question of how Christian people should respond.

This kind of activity moves people from sharing about their own immediate life experiences to the needs of the society around them. In the process they may well discover that the needs of society are intimately related to their own lives. Some possible topics:

- Hunger
- The homeless
- Nuclear weapons
- Illegal drugs
- Jails and prisons
- Crime
- Alcohol
- Suicide
- Animal rights
- Air pollution
- Water pollution
- Child abuse

Discussion on such topics as the above can be an important group activity. You do not, however, want to make the sharing and prayer time into another hour of study.

Concentrate on these issues from a Christian perspective, and look especially at the ways in which the concerns affect group members.

16. Make a group project of rewriting the Ten Commandments for our time. You can find them in Exodus 20:1–17 or Deuteronomy 5:6–21. As you discuss them, put the major emphasis on how group members see the commandments applying to their daily lives.

17. Have group members leave their shoes at the door as they enter for the meeting. Read Exodus 3:1–6 which describes Moses at the burning bush. Then talk together about the ways in which the ground where your group meets is holy ground.

18. Read about the golden calf in Exodus 32. The calf or young bull was a symbol of fertility in the nature religions of the ancient Near East. The Hebrew people broke their covenant by making the golden calf. Have group members share the things that they find are idols in their own lives. In what ways do we all break our covenant with God?

19. Read about the betrayal of Samson by Delilah in Judges 16. Have group members who are willing share times they have felt betrayed by a good friend or loved one. What weaknesses or secrets do people have which they fear might destroy them if found out by others (like Samson's secret about his hair)? This discussion can do a great deal to strengthen a group, but it is only for groups which have already achieved some confidence in one another.

20. Read the story of David and Goliath in 1 Samuel 17:31–49. Then have group members talk about contemporary situations for which they need great courage. Talk about faith in God as a source of courage.

21. Ecclesiastes 3:1–15 lists many times: a time to be born, a time to die; a time to plant, a time to pluck up what is planted; a time to kill, a time to heal; a time to break down, a time to build up; . . . a time to weep, a time to laugh; . . . Read the full passage, and then have group members share what "times" they are experiencing at the present point in their lives.

22. List on newsprint or chalkboard those who are blessed according to Beatitudes (Matthew 5:1–12):
 • The poor in spirit
 • Those who mourn
 • The meek
 • Those who hunger and thirst for righteousness
 • The merciful
 • The pure in heart
 • The peacemakers
 • Those who are persecuted for righteousness' sake

Then have each group member identify: (1) the Beatitude which he or she most strongly identifies with; (2) the Beatitude which he or she has the most difficulty embodying; (3) the Beatitude which he or she feels our contemporary society most needs practiced. Talk about the reasons for the responses.

23. Read John 13:1–15. Talk together about the implications of this passage for group life and for life in contemporary society. Jesus says:

"If I then, your Lord and Teacher, have washed your feet, you also ought to wash one another's feet" (v. 14).

Consider the possibility of a foot-washing service for your group. Youth groups respond very positively to this activity. If such a service is not part of your denominational tradition, you may find adults initially uncomfortable; but it can be an extremely moving experience. It's made easier by darkening the room—perhaps using only candle-light. Use a wide pan with only a small amount of water. You'll need towels for use by the person actually doing the foot washing. The washing should be symbolic and not too lengthy. You may well want to combine the foot washing with the sharing of communion.

24. Read about spiritual gifts in 1 Corinthians 12:1–31. Note especially the analogy to the human body in verses 14–26. Have each group member share what part of the human body he or she most strongly identifies with in terms of service to the church and to others.

25. Read John 1:1–14, the familiar prologue to the Gospel. Talk about the way in which "the Word became flesh" in Jesus Christ. Since we are part of the body of Christ, how does the Word becoming flesh affect us? Then have each group member share what he or she thinks it means for the Word to become flesh in our time.

26. Read Philippians 3:12–16. In this passage Paul advises us to forget "what lies behind" and "press on toward the goal for the prize of the upward call of God in Christ Jesus." Have each person share what things he or she needs to leave behind; resentment, destructive habits, jealousy, greed, anger, prejudice, unfulfilled dreams, or other barriers to the Christian life. Then talk about what members feel it means to "press on toward the goal."

27. Colossians 3:12–17 urges us to "put on" certain virtues and to act in affirming ways toward one another. Have each member share which of the following virtues he or she most needs to cultivate:

- compassion
- kindness
- lowliness
- meekness
- patience
- forbearing others and forgiving
- love

Paul tells the Colossians: "Let the peace of Christ rule in your hearts." What would it mean for the members of your group if the peace of Christ truly ruled in their hearts?

28. Read James 3:1–12, which talks about problems with the tongue. Then discuss these questions in your group:

- When have the tongues of others caused you pain?
- When have you been guilty of words which hurt others?
- Why does James say that no human being can tame the tongue? How can God help us control the words that we speak?

29. Read James 2:14–26, which talks about the relationship between faith and works. Through the centuries Christians have struggled to understand the proper perspective on faith and works. The Bible teaches that we are saved by faith, not works; but if our faith is real, then surely that should be reflected in our works. This passage in James was directed to people who were not concerned enough with the quality of their works or who didn't respond as they should to persons in obvious need. For group sharing:

- In what ways do we sometimes function as though we could somehow "earn" our salvation through our works? What is wrong with that attitude?
- In what ways should our faith in Christ affect how we interact with others?
- If all Christian people took seriously their faith in Christ and the resulting responsibilities, what would the impact be on problems like world hunger?
- What specific changes should we make as individuals and as a church to be more responsive to the message of James?

30. Read the beautiful words about love in 1 Corinthians 13. Ask group members to share why they feel this passage has been a favorite of many people. Then discuss:

- To whom do you most need to show love at this point in your life? Why?
- From whom do you most need to receive love at this point in your life? Why?
- Why are patience and kindness signs of love?
- In what ways are faith and hope dependent on love?
- What things do we only see dimly now?
- How can God's love transform us?